FRENCH LOVE POEMS

Also by Alistair Elliot

FRENCH LOVE POEMS

TRANSLATED BY
ALISTAIR ELLIOT

ERIC BLOOD AXE

BLOODAXE BOOKS

ISBN: 1 85224 169 1

First published 1991 by
Bloodaxe Books Ltd,
P.O. Box 1SN,
Newcastle upon Tyne NE99 1SN.

Bloodaxe Books Ltd acknowledges
the financial assistance of Northern Arts.

Cover reproduction by V & H Reprographics, Newcastle upon Tyne.

Cover printing by Index Print, Newcastle upon Tyne.

Printed in Great Britain by
Bell & Bain Limited, Glasgow, Scotland.

for
'*my wife Barbara*
who is learning Greek'

CONTENTS

FRENCH LOVE POEMS

Les Chercheuses de poux

Quand le front de l'enfant, plein de rouges tourmentes,
Implore l'essaim blanc des rêves indistincts,
Il vient près de son lit deux grandes sœurs charmantes
Avec de frêles doigts aux ongles argentins.

Elles assoient l'enfant devant une croisée
Grande ouverte où l'air bleu baigne un fouillis de fleurs,
Et dans ses lourds cheveux où tombe la rosée
Promènent leurs doigts fins, terribles et charmeurs.

Il écoute chanter leurs haleines craintives
Qui fleurent de longs miels végétaux et rosés,
Et qu'interrompt parfois un sifflement, salives
Reprises sur la lèvre ou désirs de baisers.

Il entend leurs cils noirs battant sous les silences
Parfumés; et leurs doigts électriques et doux
Font crépiter parmi ses grises indolences
Sous leurs ongles royaux la mort des petits poux.

Voilà que monte en lui le vin de la Paresse,
Soupir d'harmonica qui pourrait délirer;
L'enfant se sent, selon la lenteur des caresses,
Sourdre et mourir sans cesse un désir de pleurer.

ARTHUR RIMBAUD
(1854-91)

Girls Looking for Lice

When the child's forehead, pinched and tortured red,
Begs for the whiteout of its swarming dreams,
Two charming sisters lift towards his bed
Their silver fingernails and delicate arms.

They sit him by a window, open wide
On tangled flowers washed in the blue of air;
Thin fingers, full of charms and terrors, glide
Where the dew falls, into his heavy hair.

He listens to their breath: its shy song blows
Through strings of honey, herbal, roseate, thick,
Broken at times by hissing – overflows
Caught on the lip or kisses bitten back.

He hears the sweep, through scented silences,
Of their dark lashes; electrical and nice
In his drunk indolence, their royal claws
Crackle upon the deaths of little lice.

His head fills with the wine of Sloth, that hum
Like a harmonica threatening harmony;
He feels, as fast or slow caresses come,
Rising and falling, a desire to cry.

ARTHUR RIMBAUD

La Cousine

L'hiver a ses plaisirs: et souvent, le dimanche,
Quand un peu de soleil jaunit la terre blanche,
Avec une cousine on sort se promener...
«Et ne vous faites pas attendre pour dîner»,
Dit la mère.
                    Et, quand on a bien, aux Tuileries,
Vu sous les arbres noirs les toilettes fleuries,
La jeune fille a froid...et vous fait observer
Que le brouillard du soir commence à se lever.

Et l'on revient, parlant du beau jour qu'on regrette,
Qui s'est passé si vite...et de flamme discrète:
Et l'on sent en rentrant, avec grand appétit,
Du bas de l'escalier, – le dindon qui rôtit.

GÉRARD DE NERVAL
(1808-55)

The Girl Cousin

Winter has pleasures too: with Sunday sun
Giving the whitened earth a yellow tone,
You step out for a walk with a girl cousin...
'And don't make us wait dinner,' mother says.

And when you've seen, outside the Tuileries,
The flowered dresses under the black trees,
The young lady feels cold,
                        and turns your eyes
To where the evening fog's begun to rise.

And you pace home, demurely flirting on
Your lovely day, how sad, how soon it's gone;
And sniff, as you come in, all hungry: there's
A smell of roasting turkey right downstairs.

GÉRARD DE NERVAL

Le Manchy

Sous un nuage frais de claire mousseline,
　　Tous les dimanches au matin,
Tu venais à la ville en manchy de rotin,
　　Par les rampes de la colline.

La cloche de l'église alertement tintait;
　　Le vent de mer berçait les cannes;
Comme une grêle d'or, aux pointes des savanes,
　　Le feu du soleil crépitait.

Le bracelet aux poings, l'anneau sur la cheville,
　　Et le mouchoir jaune aux chignons,
Deux Telingas portaient, assidus compagnons,
　　Ton lit aux nattes de Manille.

Ployant leur jarret maigre et nerveux, et chantant,
　　Souples dans leurs tuniques blanches,
Le bambou sur l'épaule et les mains sur les hanches,
　　Ils allaient le long de l'Étang.

Le long de la chaussée et des varangues basses
　　Où les vieux créoles fumaient,
Par les groupes joyeux des Noirs, ils s'animaient
　　Au bruit des bobres Madécasses.

Dans l'air léger flottait l'odeur des tamarins;
　　Sur les houles illuminées,
Au large, les oiseaux, en d'immenses traînées,
　　Plongeaient dans les brouillards marins.

Et tandis que ton pied, sorti de la babouche,
　　Pendait, rose, au bord du manchy,
À l'ombre des Bois-noirs touffus et du Letchi
　　Aux fruits moins pourprés que ta bouche;

Tandis qu'un papillon, les deux ailes en fleur,
　　Teinté d'azur et d'écarlate,
Se posait par instants sur ta peau délicate
　　En y laissant de sa couleur;

The Palanquin

In a thin cloud of cool and glowing muslin
    You would come down
The hill-slopes in a palanquin of rattan
    On Sunday mornings into town.

The church bell would be tapping out its warning,
    The sea wind stroking fields of cane;
Like golden hail, the crackling fire of sunlight
    Beat on the tassels of the plain.

With bracelets on both wrists, and rings on ankles,
    And yellow kerchiefs in their plaits,
Your two Telingas, constant followers, carried
    Your bed with its Manila mats.

Flickering lean and sinewy hams, unhindered
    By their white tunics, with a song
They'd go, with hands on hips, bamboo on shoulders,
    To the Lagoon and then along –

Along the causeway by the low verandas
    Where the old creoles sat to smoke,
They'd quicken, hearing Malagasy music,
    Past groups of black men howling at a joke.

In the light air the smell of tamarinds floated;
    And on the backlit swell, always,
Far out, the endless skeins of seabirds diving
    Into the deep-sea haze.

Sometimes your foot, escaping from its slipper,
    Hung, pink, over the hammock's edges,
In the thick shade of black-wood trees and bushes
    With fruit less purple than your mouth, the litchis;

Sometimes a butterfly with flowering wings,
    Patterned bright red and blue,
Would light a moment on the delicate skin,
    Transferring colours onto you,

On voyait, au travers du rideau de batiste,
    Tes boucles dorer l'oreiller,
Et, sous leurs cils mi-clos, feignant de sommeiller,
    Tes beaux yeux de sombre améthyste.

Tu t'en venais ainsi, par ces matins si doux,
    De la montagne à la grand'messe,
Dans ta grâce naïve et ta rose jeunesse,
    Au pas rhythmé de tes Hindous.

Maintenant, dans le sable aride de nos grèves,
    Sous les chiendents, au bruit des mers,
Tu reposes parmi les morts qui me sont chers,
    O charme de mes premiers rêves!

CHARLES-MARIE-RENÉ LECONTE DE LISLE
(1818-94)

While one half-saw your curls against the pillow
    Shine golden through the curtains of batiste,
And under half-closed eyelids, as if drowsy,
    Your lovely eyes' dark amethyst.

So you would come, those sweet and peaceful mornings,
    Rocked by your Hindoos' rhythmic pace,
Out of the mountains for Communion, rosy
    With youth and full of native grace.

O charm of my first daydreams, now you lie
    With couch-grass overhead,
In barren sands, by groaning northern seas,
    At rest among my dearest dead.

LECONTE DE LISLE

Fantaisie

Il est un air pour qui je donnerais
Tout Rossini, tout Mozart, et tout Weber,
Un air très vieux, languissant et funèbre,
Qui pour moi seul a des charmes secrets!

Or, chaque fois que je viens à l'entendre,
De deux cents ans mon âme rajeunit...
C'est sous Louis treize; et je crois voir s'étendre
Un coteau vert, que le couchant jaunit,

Puis un château de brique à coins de pierre,
Aux vitraux teints de rougeâtres couleurs,
Ceint de grands parcs, avec une rivière
Baignant ses pieds, qui coule entre des fleurs;

Puis une dame, à sa haute fenêtre,
Blonde aux yeux noirs, en ses habits anciens,
Que, dans une autre existence peut-être,
J'ai déjà vue...et dont je me souviens!

GÉRARD DE NERVAL
(1808-55)

A Fancy

There is a tune for which I'd offer all
Of Mozart, all of Weber, all Rossini,
An old old tune with a darkly dying fall
And a magic it conceals except from me.

For suddenly, when I hear it played by someone,
My heart grows younger by two hundred years:
It's Louis Treize's reign, and there appears
A green slope yellowed by the evening sun;

A castle made of brick, the corners stone,
With stained-glass windows – there's a reddish gleam –
Surrounded by great parks, and with a stream
Washing its feet, with flowers all overgrown;

And a lady, at a casement in a tower,
Fair with dark eyes, in her old-fashioned dress,
Whom, in some other previous life, doubtless,
I've seen before – and I remember her!

GÉRARD DE NERVAL

Renaud le tueur de femmes

Renaud a de si grands appas
Qu'il a charmé la fille au Roi.
L'a bien emmenée à sept lieu's,
Sans qu'il lui dit un mot ou deux.

Quand sont venus à mi-chemin:
«Mon Dieu! Renaud, que j'ai grand' faim!»
«Mangez, la belle, votre main,
Car plus ne mangerez de pain.»

Quand sont venus au bord du bois:
«Mon Dieu! Renaud, que j'ai grand soif!»
«Buvez, la belle, votre sang,
Car plus ne boirez de vin blanc.»

«Il y a là-bas un vivier
Où treize dames sont noyé's,
Treize dames y sont noyé's,
La quatorzième vous serez.»

Quand sont venus près du vivier,
Lui dit de se déshabiller.
«N'est pas affaire aux chevaliers
De voir dame déshabiller.

«Mets ton épé' dessous tes pieds,
Et ton manteau devant ton nez.»
Mit son épé' dessous ses pieds
Et son manteau devant son nez.

La bell' l'a pris, l'a embrassé,
Dans le vivier ell' l'a jeté:
«Venez, anguill's, venez, poissons,
Manger la chair de ce larron!»

Renaud voulut se rattraper
À une branche de laurier;
La belle tire son epé',
Coupe la branche de laurier.

Renaud the Woman-killer

Renaud is such a handsome thing
He's charmed the daughter of the King.
He's taken her seven leagues away
And barely had one word to say.

When they had ridden nearly half,
'Oh God, Renaud, I'm all but starved!'
'My beauty, lift your hand and bite –
You'll get no more white bread to eat.'

When they had reached the edge of the forest,
'Oh God, Renaud, I've such a thirst!'
'My beauty, drink your blood this time –
You've drunk your last of cool white wine.

'In the fish-pond there, in that dead ground,
Thirteen ladies are lying drowned.
Thirteen ladies came here to drown,
And you shall be the fourteenth one.'

When they had reached the fish-pond ooze,
He told her to take off her clothes.
'No gentleman that rides a horse
Would watch a lady undo her clothes.

'Put down your sword beside your feet,
And hold your cloak across your cheek.'
He put his sword beside his feet.
He held his cloak across his cheek.

The bonny lass took him, her arms went round,
She hoyed him out into the pond:
'Come here you eels, come here you fish,
Swim up and eat this reiver's flesh!'

Renaud to save himself had managed
To grab the end of a laurel branch.
The bonny lass draws her sword and pow!
Cuts off the end of the laurel bough.

«Belle, prêtez-moi votre main,
Je vous épouserai demain!»
«Va-t’en, Renaud, va-t’en au fond
Épouser les dames qu’y sont!»

«Belle, qui vous ramènera,
Si me laissez dans ce lieu-là?»
«Ce sera ton cheval grison,
Qui suit fort bien le postillon.»

«Belle, que diront vos parents,
Quand vous verront sans votre amant?»
«Leur dirai que j’ai fait de toi
Ce que voulais faire de moi!»

ANONYMOUS BALLAD,
17TH CENTURY,
NORTHERN FRENCH (LANGUE D’OÏL)

RENAUD LE TUEUR DE FEMMES

'Oh beauty, let me have your hand.
I'll wed you tomorrow on dry land.'
'Go down, Renaud, go down and down,
Marry the ladies who lie drowned!'

'Oh beauty, who will lead you back
If you leave me here in this foul muck?'
'I shall ride home your dapple-grey;
He follows the boy and knows the way.'

'O beauty, what will your parents say
When they see you've lost your fiancé?'
'I'll tell them that I've done to thee
What thou wert gannin to do wi me!'

ANONYMOUS BALLAD

La Géante

Du temps que la Nature en sa verve puissante
Concevait chaque jour des enfants monstrueux,
J'eusse aimé vivre auprès d'une jeune géante,
Comme aux pieds d'une reine un chat voluptueux.

J'eusse aimé voir son corps fleurir avec son âme
Et grandir librement dans ses terribles jeux;
Deviner si son cœur couve une sombre flamme
Aux humides brouillards qui nagent dans ses yeux;

Parcourir à loisir ses magnifiques formes;
Ramper sur le versant de ses genoux énormes,
Et parfois en été, quand les soleils malsains,

Lasse, la font s'étendre à travers la campagne,
Dormir nonchalamment à l'ombre de ses seins,
Comme un hameau paisible au pied d'une montagne.

Charles Baudelaire
(1821-67)

The Giantess

Long, long ago, when Nature had some zest
And mothered monsters and was not effete,
I would have loved to live with a young giantess,
Like a voluptuous cat at a queen's feet.

Oh to have watched her soul begin to flower! – her size
Increasing wantonly in dreadful games;

To guess from misty looks and swimming eyes
Her heart was brooding maybe some dark flame;

To cross her magnificent contours as I pleased;

Crawl on the slope of her enormous knees;

And sometimes, when unhealthy suns had laid
Her length across the landscape, dazed with heat,
To sleep untroubled in her breasts' warm shade,
Like a calm hamlet at a mountain's feet.

CHARLES BAUDELAIRE

Tircis et Amarante
(pour Mademoiselle de Sillery)

Amenons des bergers; et puis nous rimerons
Ce que disent entre eux les Loups et les Moutons.

Tircis disoit un jour à la jeune Amarante:
«Ah! si vous connoissiez, comme moi, certain mal
   Qui nous plaît et qui nous enchante!
Il n'est bien sous le ciel qui vous parût égal.
   Souffrez qu'on vous le communique;
   Croyez-moi, n'ayez point de peur:
Voudrois-je vous tromper, vous pour qui je me pique
Des plus doux sentiments que puisse avoir un coeur?»
   Amarante aussitôt réplique:
«Comment l'appelez-vous, ce mal? quel est son nom?
– L'amour. – Ce mot est beau; dites-moi quelques marques
À quoi je le pourrai connoître: que sent-on?
– Des peines près de qui le plaisir des monarques
Est ennuyeux et fade: on s'oublie, on se plaît
   Toute seule en une forêt.
   Se mire-t-on près un rivage,
Ce n'est pas soi qu'on voit; on ne voit qu'une image
Qui sans cesse revient, et qui suit en tous lieux:
   Pour tout le reste on est sans yeux.
   Il est un berger du village
Dont l'abord, dont la voix, dont le nom fait rougir:
   On soupire à son souvenir;
On ne sait pas pourquoi, cependant on soupire;
On a peur de le voir, encor qu'on le desire.»
   Amarante dit à l'instant:
«Oh! oh! c'est là ce mal que vous me prêchez tant?
Il ne m'est pas nouveau: je pense le connoître.»

Thyrsis and Amaranta

(Fables, VIII, 13)

Let's bring some shepherds on for now, and rhyme
The talk of wolves and sheep some other time.

Thyrsis last Sunday was improving Amaranta's
    Young mind: 'I wish you knew
This illness that I have – you'd want to have it too –
    It pleases and enchants us –
  There's nothing good, this side of heaven, to match it.
    Please let me help you catch it –
    Believe me, don't be scared – be bold.
Would I trick *you*? – for whom I'm proud to say
I have the kindest feelings any heart can hold.'

    She answered straight away:
'What is this illness called? It has a name, I guess?'
  'Amour.' 'A pretty word. Tell me some things
  To know it by – the symptoms, more or less.'
  'You get such pains the ecstasy of kings
  Is dull and boring in comparison
    With this condition.
  You quite forget yourself – you could
Be happy, solitary in a wood.
  You lean and look into a stream:
You don't see you, you only see this dream
Which recurs everywhere and endlessly.
Except for that, you have no eyes to see.
  There is a shepherd, where you're from,
    The sight or voice of whom,
  Even the name, can make you blush.
You think of him, your breath comes in a rush:
    You sigh; you don't know why;
      And yet you sigh,
Afraid you'll see him, though you long to see him.'

Here Amaranta gives a little scream:
'Oh that's the illness that you praise sky-high!
It isn't new to me: I think I know it.'

Tircis à son but croyoit être,
Quand la belle ajouta: «Voilà tout justement
   Ce que je sens pour Clidamant.»
L'autre pensa mourir de dépit et de honte.

   Il est force gens comme lui,
Qui prétendent n'agir que pour leur propre compte,
   Et qui font le marché d'autrui.

JEAN DE LA FONTAINE
(1621-95)

Thyrsis, the shepherd poet,
Thinks now he's hit the target that he fancies –
When the girl adds, 'That shyness in a trance is
Exactly what I feel for Clidamantes.'

Poor fellow thought he'd die of shame and chagrin.
  He's not alone, though. Lots imagine
They're acting for themselves, and then discover
They've done the bargaining for some other lover.

JEAN DE LA FONTAINE

Le Tombeau de Marmousette

Il faut que ma triste Musette,
O Noble et divine Catin,
Souspire le cruel Destin
De vostre pauvre Marmousette;
Il faut que soubs ce vieux Cyprez,
Qui fournit la Parque de traits,
Je deplore sa fin estrange,
Et que le dueil en soit si beau,
Que de la Seine jusqu'au Gange
L'on puisse envier son Tombeau.

Sus venez donc en cette place,
Non les Chiens vilains et hargneux,
Mais bien les gentils Espagneux,
Pleindre l'honneur de vostre Race;
Venez pousser autour de moy
L'esclat d'un si funeste abboy,
Que l'impiteuse Canicule,
Avec un long ressentiment,
Pour hurler comme vous, s'accule
Contre l'Azur du Firmament.

Qu'elle ne soit pas toute seule
A vous respondre en cét ennuy,
Mais qu'à mesme effet aujourd'huy
Cerbere ouvre sa triple gueule.
Las! ce noir Portier des Enfers,
Au col chargé d'horribles fers,
A des-ja veu là bas son Ombre;
Elle a des-ja foulé le bord,
Où vont dans cét Empire sombre
Les Chiens heureux apres la mort.

O trop lamantable advanture!
A peine six fois le Croissant
L'avoit esclairée en naissant,
Qu'elle a trouvé sa sepulture;
Ses yeux si gays, et si jolys,
Son corps qui faisoit honte aux Lys,

The Grave of Marmousette

My little bagpipe-Muse, Musette,
O noble Catherine, divine Kate,
Is duty-bound to mourn the fate
Of your wee dog, poor Marmousette.
So under this old cypress tree,
A source of darts for Destiny,
I'll weep for her strange end, a theme
For such a ravishing lament
That all from Seine to Ganges' stream
Will envy her this monument.

Come to this tree, this tearful place –
None of you nasty snarling mongrels
From nowhere, just you gentle Spaniels,
To mourn the honour of your race.
Come sit by me and bark to say
Our sorrow in the plainest way,
Until the pitiless Dog-Star burns
To answer and, to howl like you,
From such long sympathy, stops and turns
At bay against the heavenly blue.

And may that Dog not be alone
To harmonise with your sad note,
But Cerberus, with his triple throat,
Must add the infernal undertone.
Alas! that black concierge, whose necks
Wear Hades' collars made of snakes,
Has seen her Shade already there,
Marking the shore on the far side,
Down in the dusky kingdom where
Lucky dogs go when they have died.

Oh what a lamentable story!
Since she was born, the crescent moon
Shone on her scarce six times: too soon
It lit her to the cemetery.
Her eyes so bright and gay, her body
Which made a lily look quite dirty,

Ses longues oreilles tannées,
Et la beauté de son maintien,
Contre les fieres Destinées,
A ses jours n'ont servy de rien.

Il est bien vray que quand on pense
A la main qui fist son trespas,
On y rencontre tant d'appas,
Que son malheur s'en recompense;
Un coup de Mail inopiné,
Fatalement luy fut donné
Par sa chere Maistresse mesme:
Hé! pouvoit-elle perir mieux,
Que par ce Miracle supreme,
De qui l'oeil fait mourir les Dieux!

Non, non, ô la Reine des charmes,
Sa gloire est sans comparaison,
Et c'est avec juste raison,
Que je veux terminer mes larmes;
Aussi bien aprés la pitié,
Qu'en tesmoigne vostre amitié,
La mienne auroit mauvaise grace;
Tay toi donc ma Musette icy,
Et dy seulement à voix basse,
Que je voudrois finir ainsi.

ANTOINE GIRARD, SIEUR DE SAINT-AMANT
(1594-1661)

Her long brown ears, the way that she
Kept herself beautiful, spick and span,
Meant nothing to fierce Destiny,
Who sticks minutely to his plan.

It's true that when one meditates
Upon the hand that did the harm,
There one encounters so much charm
The damage ends – it compensates.
A croquet mall drawn smartly back
Surprised her with a fatal smack:
It was her mistress' hand that struck.
Ah! could she find a better death
Than from this Miracle, whose look
Causes the gods to lose their breath?

No no, Your Highness, Queen of Chic,
Her glory is beyond compare:
There is no cause for mourning there;
So I shall sigh, and dry my cheek.
Besides, when You show such regret
And thus Your passion for Your pet,
It's graceless to express my own.
Now, little bagpipe, cease to play –
But folded, mutter through a drone
That I should like to end that way.

ANTOINE GIRARD, SIEUR DE SAINT-AMANT

Sonnets pour Hélène

(I, 22)

Puis qu'elle est toute hyver, toute la mesme glace,
Toute neige, & son cœur tout armé de glaçons, ·
Qui ne m'aime sinon pour avoir mes chansons,
Pourquoy suis-je si fol que je ne m'en délace?
Dequoy me sert son nom, sa grandeur & sa race,
Que d'honneste servage & de belles prisons?
Maistresse, je n'ay pas les cheveux si grisons,
Qu'une autre de bon cœur ne prenne vostre place.
Amour, qui est enfant, ne cele verité.
Vous n'estes si superbe, ou si riche en beauté,
Qu'il faille desdaigner un bon cœur qui vous aime.
R'entrer en mon Avril desormais je ne puis:
Aimez moy s'il vous plaist, grison comme je suis,
Et je vous aimeray quand vous serez de mesme.

(II,42)

Quand vous serez bien vieille, au soir à la chandelle,
Assise aupres du feu, devidant & filant,
Direz chantant mes vers, en vous esmerveillant,
Ronsard me celebroit du temps que j'estois belle.
Lors vous n'aurez servante oyant telle nouvelle,
Desja sous le labeur à demy sommeillant,
Qui au bruit de mon nom ne s'aille resveillant,
Benissant vostre nom de louange immortelle.
Je seray sous la terre: & fantôme sans os
Par les ombres myrteux je prendray mon repos:
Vous serez au fouyer une vieille accroupie,
Regrettant mon amour & vostre fier desdain.
Vivez, si m'en croyez, n'attendez à demain:
Cueillez dés aujourd'huy les roses de la vie.

PIERRE DE RONSARD
(1524-85)

Sonnets for Helen

(I, 22)

Since she's all winter, with a heart of snow
Plated in ice and armed with icicles,
And loves me only for these canticles,
I'm mad not to undo my bonds and go.
   What use to me are her great name and race? –
Beautiful prisons, well-bred slavery.
– Mistress, my hair's not gone so grey on me
Another heart won't gladly take your place.

Love is a child and does not hide the truth:
You may be proud, and rich in beauty too,
But not enough to scorn a heart that's true;
   I can't re-enter April and my youth.
Grey though my head is now, love me today,
And I shall love you when your own is grey.

(II, 42)

When you are old, and sitting, candle-lit,
Close to the fire, teasing and spinning wool,
You'll sing my lines and, wondering, admit,
'Ronsard praised me, when I was beautiful.'

Then what young servant of that future house,
To hear of you and Ronsard, will not raise
Her drooping head from work, start from her drowse
And bless your name for that immortal praise.

I shall be fleshless, ghostly under earth,
Among the lovers' shades at last at rest,
You an old woman bent beside the hearth
Regretting that I loved and you said Nay.
   Live now, don't wait, don't think tomorrow's best:
Gather the roses of this life today.

PIERRE DE RONSARD

Nevermore

Souvenir, souvenir, que me veux-tu? L'automne
Faisait voler la grive à travers l'air atone,
Et le soleil dardait un rayon monotone
Sur le bois jaunissant où la bise détonne.

Nous étions seul à seule et marchions en rêvant,
Elle et moi, les cheveux et la pensée au vent.
Soudain, tournant vers moi son regard émouvant:
«Quel fut ton plus beau jour?» fit sa voix d'or vivant,

Sa voix douce et sonore, au frais timbre angélique.
Un sourire discret lui donna la réplique,
Et je baisai sa main blanche, dévotement.

– Ah! les premières fleurs, qu'elles sont parfumées!
Et qu'il bruit avec un murmure charmant
Le premier *oui* qui sort de lèvres bien-aimées!

PAUL VERLAINE
(1844-96)

Nevermore

Memory, why torment me? Autumn skimmed
A struggling thrush through the dull air. The sun
Darted a colourless wand of light upon
The yellowing wood which thunders in the wind.

We were alone, and as we walked we dreamed,
Our hair and thoughts both flying in the breeze.
And then she turned to me her touching eyes:
'What was your loveliest day?' – her golden sound,

Her sweet voice, deep, with a fresh angelic ring.
A tactful smile was all I need reply,
And kissing her white hand – religiously.

– Oh, the first flowers – what a scent they have!
And what a charm breathes in the murmuring
Of the first *yes* that comes from lips you love!

PAUL VERLAINE

37

À Vénus

Ayant apres long desir
Pris de ma doulce ennemie
Quelques arres du plaisir
Que sa rigueur me denie,

Je t'offre ces beaux œillets,
Venus, je t'offre ces roses,
Dont les boutons vermeillets
Imitent les levres closes,

Que j'ay baisé par trois fois,
Marchant tout beau dessoubs l'ombre
De ce buisson, que tu vois:
Et n'ay sceu passer ce nombre,

Pource que la mere estoit
Aupres de là, ce me semble,
Laquelle nous aguettoit:
De peur encores j'en tremble.

Or' je te donne des fleurs:
Mais si tu fais ma rebelle
Autant piteuse à mes pleurs
Comme à mes yeux elle est belle,

Un Myrte je dediray
Dessus les rives de Loyre,
Et sur l'écorse escriray
Ces quatre vers à ta gloire:

THENOT SUR CE BORD ICY,
À VENUS SACRE ET ORDONNE
CE MYRTE ET LUY DONNE AUSSI
CES TROPPEAUX ET SA PERSONNE.

JOACHIM DU BELLAY
(1522-60)

38

To Venus

Having after long desire
Won from my sweet enemy
Some advance on that delight
Her cruelty refuses me,

Venus, here I offer you
Pink and rose and violet,
Flowers whose little scarlet buds
Look so like her lips, still shut,

Lips that I have kissed three times,
Walking softly to her door
In the shadow of this bush –
And I couldn't kiss her more:

For I thought her mother hid
Listening to us somewhere near,
Watching everything we did –
I am trembling still with fear.

Now I give you only flowers;
But if you turn her sympathies,
And make her kindly to my tears
As she's lovely in my eyes,

Then I'll dedicate to you
By the Loire a myrtle tree,
And in your honour cut the bark
With these lines of poetry:

Thenot consecrated here
To Venus, on these river banks,
This myrtle; also all these flocks,
And himself, in grateful thanks.

JOACHIM DU BELLAY

«Elle était déchaussée, elle était décoiffée»

Elle était déchaussée, elle était décoiffée,
Assise, les pieds nus, parmi les joncs penchants;
Moi qui passais par là, je crus voir une fée,
Et je lui dis: Veux-tu t'en venir dans les champs?

Elle me regarda de ce regard suprême
Qui reste à la beauté quand nous en triomphons,
Et je lui dis: Veux-tu, c'est le mois où l'on aime,
Veux-tu nous en aller sous les arbres profonds?

Elle essuya ses pieds à l'herbe de la rive;
Elle me regarda pour la seconde fois,
Et la belle folâtre alors devint pensive.
Oh! comme les oiseaux chantaient au fond des bois!

Comme l'eau caressait doucement le rivage!
Je vis venir à moi, dans les grands roseaux verts,
La belle fille heureuse, effarée et sauvage,
Ses cheveux dans ses yeux, et riant au travers.

VICTOR HUGO
(1802-85)

'She had no shoes on'

She had no shoes on, she had freed her hair,
Sitting bare-legged among the drooping reeds.
As I passed by, I thought I'd seen a fairy;
I said: Come out, come with me to the fields.

She looked at me, she looked with that far-off
High look, that even conquered beauties keep;
I said: Come out, this is the month of love –
Shall we go that way, where the trees are deep?

She wiped her feet against the bankside grass.
She looked at me again, her playful mood
And beauty changing into thoughtfulness.
Oh how the birds were singing in the wood...

How softly the small river lipped its edge...
Then she was coming, happy and afraid,
Towards me, wild and fair, through spears of sedge,
Hair in her eyes, and smiling not quite straight.

VICTOR HUGO

Antoine et Cléopâtre

Tous deux ils regardaient, de la haute terrasse,
L'Egypte s'endormir sous un ciel étouffant
Et le Fleuve, à travers le Delta noir qu'il fend,
Vers Bubaste ou Saïs rouler son onde grasse.

Et le Romain sentait sous la lourde cuirasse,
Soldat captif berçant le sommeil d'un enfant,
Ployer et défaillir sur son cœur triomphant
Le corps voluptueux que son étreinte embrasse.

Tournant sa tête pâle entre ses cheveux bruns
Vers celui qu'enivraient d'invincibles parfums,
Elle tendit sa bouche et ses prunelles claires;

Et sur elle courbé, l'ardent Imperator
Vit dans ses larges yeux étoilés de points d'or
Toute une mer immense où fuyaient des galères.

José-Maria de Heredia
(1842-1905)

Antony and Cleopatra

Together they stood watching on the terrace
As Egypt fell asleep under a stifling heaven
And the Nile rolled its fatness down to cleave
Its own black delta, to Sais or to Bubastis.

The Roman soldier, now a prisoner caught
Nursing a sleepy child, under the weight of his cuirass
Feels the luxurious body he embraces
Bend and give way on his triumphant heart.

Turning her face, pale in brown hair, to meet
This man half-drunk on her invincible scents,
Now she holds up her mouth and her clear eyes;

Bent over her the Imperator sees
In her wide pupils starred with golden points
An immeasurable sea with ships in flight.

JOSÉ-MARIA DE HEREDIA

Les Pas

Tes pas, enfants de mon silence,
Saintement, lentement placés,
Vers le lit de ma vigilance
Procèdent, muets et glacés.

Personne pure, ombre divine,
Qu'ils sont doux, tes pas retenus!
Dieux!...tous les dons que je devine
Viennent à moi sur ces pieds nus!

Si, de tes lèvres avancées,
Tu prépares pour l'apaiser,
À l'habitant de mes pensées
La nourriture d'un baiser,

Ne hâte pas cet acte tendre,
Douceur d'être et de n'être pas,
Car j'ai vécu de vous attendre,
Et mon cœur n'était que vos pas.

PAUL VALÉRY
(1871-1945)

44

The Footsteps

Your steps, born of my silence here,
Process with slow, religious tread,
Dumbly and icily, to where
I lie awake, on watch, in bed.

Pure person, shade of deity,
Your steps, held back, are doubly sweet.
God! – all the gifts I could foresee
Are coming now on those bare feet!

If you advance your lips to make
A peace with hunger, and to press
The inhabitant of my thoughts to take
The thoughtful nourishment of a kiss,

Don't hurry with their tender dew,
Sweetness complete and incomplete;
For I have lived to wait for you:
My heart was your approaching feet.

PAUL VALÉRY

Élégie XIX

Sans ame, sans esprit, sans pouls, & sans haleine,
Je n'avois ny tendon, ny artere, ny veine,
Qui dissoute ne fust du combat amoureux.
Mes yeux estoient couverts d'un voile tenebreux,
Mes oreilles tintoient, & ma langue seichée
Estoit à mon palais de chaleur attachée.
A bras demi-tombez ton col j'entrelaçois:
Nul vent de mes poulmons pasmé je ne poussois:
J'avois devant les yeux ce royaume funeste
Qui jamais ne jouist de la clairté celeste,
(Royaume que Pluton pour partage a voulu)
Et de vieillard Caron le bateau vermoulu.
Bref j'estois demi-mort, quand tes poulmons s'enflerent,
Et d'une tiede haleine en souspirant soufflerent
Un baiser en ma bouche entrecoupé des coups
De ta langue lezarde, & de ton ris si doux:
Baiser vivifiant, nourricier de mon ame,
Dont l'alme, douce, humide, & restaurante flame
Esloigna de mes yeux mon trespas & ma nuict,
Et feit que le bateau du vieillard qui conduit
Les ames des amans à la rive amoureuse,
S'en alla sans passer la mienne langoureuse.
Ainsi ju fus guary par l'esprit d'un baiser:
Je ne veux plus Maistresse, à tel prix appaiser
Ma chaleur Cyprienne, & mesmement à l'heure
Que le Soleil ardent sous la Chienne demeure,
Et que son chaud rayon sur nos testes jetté
Brusle tout nostre sang, & renflame l'Esté.
En ce temps faisons tréve, espargnons nostre vie:
De peur que mal-armez de la Philosophie
Nous ne sentions soudain, ou apres à loisir,
Que tousjours la douleur voisine le plaisir.

PIERRE DE RONSARD
(1524-85)

Elegy XIX
(A Kiss)

Without a soul, a mind, a breath, or pulse,
I held no strings of arteries, veins or muscles –
All had untied themselves in love's hot fight.
A veil of darkness bandaged up my sight,
My ears had started ringing, my tongue dried
And stuck with heat to some cave-roof inside,
My arms half-fallen-off ensnared your throat,
I fainted, lungs too weak to vent a note,
That gloomy kingdom swam before my eyes
Which never knows the heavenly joy of skies,
I saw the kingdom that King Pluto chose,
And worm-holes in the boat old Charon rows.
In short, half-dead, I felt your lungs inflate
And with a warmly sighing breath translate
Into my mouth a kiss, soon broken up among
Sweet puffs of laughter and your darting lizard tongue –
A kiss that fed my soul and made me live,
A sweet kind flame, moist and restorative,
That banished death and darkness from my eyelids
And made the boat of the old man who guides
The souls of lovers to the shore of love,
Leave without taking mine – too ill to move.
So I was cured by the spirit of a kiss.
   Let's stop appeasing (at a cost like this)
My Cyprian heat, dear heart, especially days
When Sol rolls underneath the Dog to blaze
And, throwing rays of sunstroke from his torch,
Burns up our blood and makes the summer scorch.
Let's make truce now, save up vitality,
For fear (ill-armed in our philosophy)
We feel too soon   or afterwards, at leisure
Anguish is always there, next door to pleasure.

PIERRE DE RONSARD

Parfum exotique

Quand, les deux yeux fermés, en un soir chaud d'automne,
Je respire l'odeur de ton sein chaleureux,
Je vois se dérouler des rivages heureux
Qu'éblouissent les feux d'un soleil monotone;

Une île paresseuse où la nature donne
Des arbres singuliers et des fruits savoureux;
Des hommes dont le corps est mince et vigoureux,
Et des femmes dont l'œil par sa franchise étonne.

Guidé par ton odeur vers de charmants climats,
Je vois un port rempli de voiles et de mâts
Encor tout fatigués par la vague marine,

Pendant que le parfum des verts tamariniers,
Qui circule dans l'air et m'enfle la narine,
Se mêle dans mon âme au chant des mariniers.

CHARLES BAUDELAIRE
(1821-67)

Exotic Scent

On a warm autumn evening, if I shut both eyes
And breathe the smell of heat from your warm breast,
I see unfolding a long happy coast
That endless sun has burnt into a daze;

An island state of sloth, where nature grows
The strangest trees, and fruits of delicate taste;
Where men are lean and strong, and women rest
Their eyes on one with startling openness.

Following your smell toward this charming zone,
I see a harbour full of masts and sails
Still shaken from the ocean waves and winds,

And then the scent of verdant tamarinds
Comes wafting to my heart and swells my nostrils,
Mixed with the shanties of the deep-sea men.

CHARLES BAUDELAIRE

Sed Non Satiata

Bizarre déité, brune comme les nuits,
Au parfum mélangé de musc et de havane,
Œuvre de quelque obi, le Faust de la savane,
Sorcière au flanc d'ébène, enfant des noirs minuits,

Je préfère au constance, à l'opium, au nuits,
L'élixir de ta bouche où l'amour se pavane;
Quand vers toi mes désirs partent en caravane,
Tes yeux sont la citerne où boivent mes ennuis.

Par ces deux grands yeux noirs, soupiraux de ton âme,
O démon sans pitié! verse-moi moins de flamme;
Je ne suis pas le Styx pour t'embrasser neuf fois,

Hélas! et je ne puis, Mégère libertine,
Pour briser ton courage et te mettre aux abois,
Dans l'enfer de ton lit devenir Proserpine!

CHARLES BAUDELAIRE
(1821-67)

She Is Not Satisfied

Outlandish idol, brown as night, who overpower
  My sense with blended musk and dry Havana,
  Work of some obi-man, some Faust of the savannah,
You witch with ebony thighs, born at the blackest hour,

I know Cape wine, opium, Côte de Nuits – but best I think
  The elixir of your mouth where love lolls, on view;
  And when the caravan of my desires sets out for you,
Your eyes are the cistern where my troubles stop and drink.

But pour me now from those two great dark eyes
  (Where your soul breathes) less flame, relentless demon:
I'm not the Styx, to give you nine embraces,

Alas! – nor, lecherous Fury, can I turn your head
  And break your last resistence by becoming
Proserpina in the Hades of your bed.

CHARLES BAUDELAIRE

À Julie

On me demande, par les rues,
Pourquoi je vais bayant aux grues,
Fumant mon cigare au soleil,
À quoi se passe ma jeunesse,
Et depuis trois ans de paresse
Ce qu'ont fait mes nuits sans sommeil.

Donne-moi tes lèvres, Julie;
Les folles nuits qui t'ont pâlie
Ont séché leur corail luisant.
Parfume-les de ton haleine;
Donne-les-moi, mon Africaine,
Tes belles lèvres de pur sang.

Mon imprimeur crie à tue-tête
Que sa machine est toujours prête,
Et que la mienne n'en peut mais.
D'honnêtes gens, qu'un club admire,
N'ont pas dédaigné de prédire
Que je n'en reviendrai jamais.

Julie, as-tu du vin d'Espagne?
Hier, nous battions la campagne;
Va donc voir s'il en reste encor.
Ta bouche est brûlante, Julie;
Inventons donc quelque folie
Qui nous perde l'âme et le corps.

On dit que ma gourme me rentre,
Que je n'ai plus rien dans le ventre,
Que je suis vide à faire peur;
Je crois, si j'en valais la peine,
Qu'on m'enverrait à Sainte-Hélène,
Avec un cancer dans le cœur.

Allons, Julie, il faut t'attendre
À me voir quelque jour en cendre,
Comme Hercule sur son rocher.
Puisque c'est par toi que j'expire,
Ouvre ta robe, Déjanire,
Que je monte sur mon bûcher.

ALFRED DE MUSSET (1810-57)

To Julie

They quiz me in the street because
I go round gaping after whores,
Puffing cigar-smoke in the sun;
What am I doing with my youth?
And after three full years of sloth,
What prizes have my white nights won?

Julie, give me your lips again:
These crazy nights untan the skin
And make their shining coral dull –
Revive them with a scented puff
Of your moist breath, my African love,
Lips of pure blood, and beautiful.

My printer shouts across the city
That his machine is always ready,
But mine's worn out. And decent men,
The prophets of small clubs, are letting
Their circles know they don't mind betting
I shan't get back the use of my pen.

Julie, got any Spanish rouge in?
Yesterday's lost in such confusion.
Go look, in case we spared a bottle.
My God, your mouth is burning, Julie;
Let's work out something mad, and really
Get wasted, absolutely mortal.

This is the crop of my wild oats,
They say; and once I had some guts;
And I've become so blank it's frightening.
I think, if I were worth the fare,
They'd send me to Napoleon's lair,
With (in my chest) a cancer beating.

Julie, you must expect some day
I'll burst in flames and burn away,
Like Hercules on his hilltop fire.
Since you're the death of me, come nearer:
Open your robe, Deianira,
So I can mount my funeral pyre.

ALFRED DE MUSSET

Jalousie

Telle qu'était Diane, alors qu'imprudemment
L'infortuné chasseur la voyait toute nue,
Telle dedans un bain Clorinde s'est tenue,
N'ayant le corps vêtu que d'un moite élément.

Quelque Dieu dans ces eaux caché secrètement
A vu tous les appas dont la belle est pourvue:
Mais s'il n'en avait eu seulement que la vue,
Je serais moins jaloux de son contentement.

Le traître, l'insolent, n'étant qu'une eau versée,
L'a baisée en tous lieux, l'a toujours embrassée;
J'enrage de colère à m'en ressouvenir.

Cependant cet objet dont je suis idolâtre,
Après tous ces excès, n'a fait pour le punir
Que donner à son onde une couleur d'albâtre.

TRISTAN L'HERMITE
(c.1601-55)

54

Jealousy

As Artemis was, when (so imprudently)
The unlucky hunter looked, and saw her bare,
So, in her bath, Clorinda held quite still,
Clothed simply in the wetness round her body.

Some god, slipped in those waters secretly,
Saw every charm she has that's visible –
But if he'd only seen them, I could bear
A god's content, without much jealousy.

The traitor, some mere jugful from the well,
Kissed her in every part, embraced her all –
I burst with rage to think of it again.

But all she did, my idol, to that bastard,
After that orgy, as a punishment,
Was – give his waves a tint of alabaster.

TRISTAN L'HERMITE

Délie

Seul avec moy, elle avec sa partie:
Moy en ma peine, elle en sa molle couche.
Couvert d'ennuy je me voultre en l'Ortie,
Et elle nue entre ses bras se couche.
    Hà (luy indigne) il la tient, il la touche:
Elle le souffre: et, comme moins robuste,
Viole amour par ce lyen injuste,
Que droict humain, et non divin, à faict.
    O saincte loy a tous, fors a moy, juste,
Tu me punys pour elle avoir meffaict.

Tout jugement de celle infinité,
Ou tout concept se trouve superflus,
Et tout aigu de perspicuité
Ne pourroyent joindre au sommet de son plus.
    Car seulement l'apparent du surplus,
Premiere neige en son blanc souveraine,
Au pur des mains delicatement saine,
Ahontiroyt le nud de Bersabée:
Et le flagrant de sa suave alaine
Apouriroyt l'odorante Sabée.

Toute fumée en forme d'une nue
Depart du feu avec grave maintien:
Mais tant plus hault s'esleve, et se denue,
Et plus soubdain se resoult toute en rien.
    Or que seroit a penetrer au bien,
Qui au parfaict d'elle jamais ne fault?
Quand seulement pensant plus, qu'il ne fault,
Et contemplant sa face a mon dommage,
L'œil, et le sens peu a peu me deffault,
Et me pers tout en sa divine image.

MAURICE SCÈVE
(c.1510-64)

Délie

Lonely and by myself – she with her fellow;
I on my rack – she in her feather bed;
Under my sheet of pain I writhe on nettles,
And she lies back between his elbows naked.
Unworthy mate! he holds her, touches her;
She suffers him; and posing as the weaker,
Violates Love in this immoral bond
Forged not in heaven but by society.
O holy Law, so just to all but me,
You punish me for her deliberate wrong!

DIZAIN 166

No reckoning of her infinity
(Where all Ideas of her wander, lost)
Nor the most piercing sight of mind or eye
Could reach the summit she has reached and passed.
For simply what she shows (from so much more),
A substance of first snow, surpassing white,
Unmarked by cleanest hands, and delicate,
Would put to shame Bathsheba's nakedness;
And the sweet breath with which she scents the air
Would turn the oils of Sheba into dust.

DIZAIN 397

Smoke aspires upward to a higher state
And leaves the fire with cloudy gravity,
But as it rises it throws off its weight
Till it dissolves to nothing suddenly.
    What would it be to sink into the good
That flows forever from her perfect centre? –
When just to think more closely than I should,
Or (to my harm) to contemplate her face,
Makes sight and sense and self desert their place –
Lost in the heavenly image that they enter.

MAURICE SCÈVE

«Non que je veuille ôter la liberté»

Non que je veuille ôter la liberté
À qui est né pour être sur moi maître:
Non que je veuille abuser de fierté,
Qui à lui humble et à tous devrais être:
Non que je veuille à dextre et à senestre
Le gouverner, et faire à mon plaisir:
Mais je voudrais, pour nos deux cœurs repaître,
Que son vouloir fût joint à mon désir.

PERNETTE DU GUILLET
(*c*.1520-45)

'Not that I'd wish to steal the liberty'

Not that I'd wish to steal the liberty
From the man born to power over me:
Not that I'd wish to play the game of pride
When what I owe him is humility:
Not that I'd wish to turn him as we ride
To left or right, to do as I require:
But I should wish, so both were satisfied,
That his strong will were joined to my desire.

PERNETTE DU GUILLET

Solo de lune

Je fume, étalé face au ciel,
Sur l'impériale de la diligence,
Ma carcasse est cahotée, mon âme danse
Comme un Ariel;
Sans miel, sans fiel, ma belle âme danse,
Ô routes, coteaux, ô fumées, ô vallons,
Ma belle âme, ah! récapitulons.

Nous nous aimions comme deux fous,
On s'est quitté sans en parler,
Un spleen me tenait exilé,
Et ce spleen me venait de tout. Bon.

Ses yeux disaient: «Comprenez-vous?
«Pourquoi ne comprenez-vous pas?»
Mais nul n'a voulu faire le premier pas,
Voulant trop tomber *ensemble* à genoux.
(Comprenez-vous?)

Où est-elle à cette heure?
Peut-être qu'elle pleure...
Où est-elle à cette heure?
Oh! du moins, soigne-toi, je t'en conjure!

Ô fraîcheur des bois le long de la route,
Ô châle de mélancolie, toute âme est un peu aux écoutes,
Que ma vie
Fait envie!
Cette impériale de diligence tient de la magie.

Accumulons l'irréparable!
Renchérissons sur notre sort!
Les étoiles sont plus nombreuses que le sable
Des mers où d'autres ont vu se baigner son corps;
Tout n'en va pas moins à la Mort,
Y a pas de port.

Solo by Moonlight

I smoke, stretched out face up
To heaven inside the rail
Around the stage-coach top,
My carcase being jolted, but my soul
Dancing like Ariel;
Clear as a bell, neither in heaven nor hell,
My sweet soul dances in my brain –
Highway and hill, and puff of smoke and dale,
Sweet soul, come on, let's have it all again.

We were in love, a crazy pair,
We parted without saying so,
I was withdrawn and rather low,
Depression rising everywhere. Okay.

Her eyes said, 'Do you understand?
Why don't you understand?'
But neither would be first to take a hand,
We had to fall *together* on our knees.
(You understand these synchronicities?)

Where is she at this minute?
Maybe in tears somewhere...
Where is she at this minute?
At least take care; look after yourself! Please!

O cool of woods along the road,
O shawl of melancholia, every soul's
A bit on edge –
Ah! how they envy me
Getting away scot-free!
This stage-coach roof! I think there's magic in it!

Let's make the irrevocable worse, increase
The odds against our destiny!
There are more stars than grains of sand in seas
Where she has swum observed by other men than me;
It all arrives at Death, however:
There's no safe harbour.

Des ans vont passer là-dessus,
On s'endurcira chacun pour soi,
Et bien souvent et déjà je m'y vois,
On se dira: «Si j'avais su...»
Mais mariés de même, ne se fût-on pas dit:
«Si j'avais su, si j'avais su!...»?
Ah! rendez-vous maudit!
Ah! mon cœur sans issue!...
Je me suis mal conduit.

Maniaques de bonheur,
Donc, que ferons-nous? Moi de mon âme,
Elle de sa faillible jeunesse?
Ô vieillissante pécheresse,
Oh! que de soirs je vais me rendre infâme
En ton honneur!

Ses yeux clignaient: «Comprenez-vous?
«Pourquoi ne comprenez-vous pas?»
Mais nul n'a fait le premier pas
Pour tomber ensemble à genoux. Ah!...

La Lune se lève,
Ô route en grand rêve!...

On a dépassé les filatures, les scieries,
Plus que les bornes kilométriques,
De petits nuages d'un rose de confiserie,
Cependant qu'un fin croissant de lune se lève,
Ô route de rêve, ô nulle musique...
Dans ces bois de pins où depuis
Le commencement du monde
Il fait toujours nuit,
Que de chambres propres et profondes!
Oh! pour un soir d'enlèvement!
Et je les peuple et je m'y vois,
Et c'est un beau couple d'amants,
Qui gesticulent hors la loi.

Years will flow over all of this,
Our skins will thicken, each alone,
And often – I can see myself already –
We shall start saying: 'If I'd known...'
But even wed, we might have said,
'If only... If I'd only known...'
Oh, damn that meeting that we had,
My heart with no way out –
My conduct has been pretty bad.

O lunatics of happiness,
What are we going to do,
I with my soul and you
With youth about to fade?
O aging sinner,
How many nights I'm going to degrade
My body in your honour!

Her eyes were blinking: 'Do you understand? No.
Why don't you understand?' But neither
Took the first step toward the other
And falling on our knees together. So!...

The rising Moon is what it seems,
The road's a line of dreams.

We've passed the sawmills and the cotton-mills,
Nothing but milestones to be seen,
And small clouds of confectionery pink,
While a lunar croissant rises, rather thin,
O road of dreams, o non-existent music...

Among these pinewoods where
It's always dark, where it has been
Dark since the world was new,
How many rooms there are,
Rooms to sink into, deep and clean.
Oh, to elope some evening there!
I fill the woods with people, I'm there too,
I see us – what a lovely loving pair!
Waving back outside the law.

Et je passe et les abandonne,
Et me recouche face au ciel,
La route tourne, je suis Ariel,
Nul ne m'attend, je ne vais chez personne,
Je n'ai que l'amitié des chambres d'hôtel.

La lune se lève,
Ô route en grand rêve!
Ô route sans terme,
Voici le relais,
Où l'on allume les lanternes,
Où l'on boit un verre de lait,
Et fouette postillon,
Dans le chant des grillons,
Sous les étoiles de juillet.

Ô clair de Lune,
Noce de feux de Bengale noyant mon infortune,
Les ombres des peupliers sur la route,...
Le gave qui s'écoute,...
Qui s'écoute chanter,...
Dans ces inondations du fleuve du Léthé,...

Ô Solo de lune,
Vous défiez ma plume,
Oh! cette nuit sur la route;
Ô Étoiles, vous êtes à faire peur,
Vous y êtes toutes! toutes!
Ô fugacité de cette heure...
Oh! qu'il y eût moyen
De m'en garder l'âme pour l'automne qui vient!...

Voici qu'il fait très très-frais,
Oh! si à la même heure,
Elle va de même le long des forêts,
Noyer son infortune
Dans les noces du clair de lune!...
(Elle aime tant errer tard!)
Elle aura oublié son foulard,
Elle va prendre mal, vu la beauté de l'heure!
Oh! soigne-toi je t'en conjure!
Oh! je ne veux plus entendre cette toux!

I pass them, leave them all behind,
And lying back, turn up my face,
The high road bends, I'm Ariel,
No one expects me, going to no one's place,
My only friends are rooms in blank hotels.

The rising moon is what it seems,
The road's a line of dreams.
The road will never end or die,
But here's the post-house where we change the horses,
And light the lamps and sip,
Till the postillion cracks his whip,
A glass of milk, with crickets singing
Under the ringing
Stars of July.

O moonlit Night,
With wedding party fireworks drowning my misfortune,
Shadows of poplars on the road of dream...
The mountain burn you hear
Singing in your ear,
Among these floods that pour from Lethe Stream...

O solo in the moonlight,
How you defy my flying pen!
The darkness on the road tonight!
O stars, you make a fearsome sight!
All present, every one of you is here!
How fast the hour turns and runs away...
If there were just some way
To keep its essence for the coming end of the year!

How cool it is, oh more than cool –
Suppose she's going too,
This very minute,
Along a forest edge to drown
Her own misfortune in the moonbeam party –
She is so fond of walking late –
She'll have forgotten to put on her scarf,
She'll catch her death considering
The beauty of the time of night,
Take care! look after yourself, please!
I do not want to hear that cough again!

Ah! que ne suis-je tombé à tes genoux!
Ah! que n'as-tu défailli à mes genoux!
J'eusse été le modèle des époux!
Comme le frou-frou de ta robe est le modèle des frou-frou.

JULES LAFORGUE
(1860-87)

Why didn't I fall at your knees?
Why didn't you just faint at mine?
I'd have been the sweetest husband you could wish,
Like the swishing of your dress being the sweetest swish...

JULES LAFORGUE

Brise marine

La chair est triste, hélas! et j'ai lu tous les livres.
Fuir! là-bas fuir! Je sens que des oiseaux sont ivres
D'être parmi l'écume inconnue et les cieux!
Rien, ni les vieux jardins reflétés par les yeux
Ne retiendra ce cœur qui dans la mer se trempe
O nuits! ni la clarté déserte de ma lampe
Sur le vide papier que la blancheur défend,
Et ni la jeune femme allaitant son enfant.
Je partirai! Steamer balançant ta mâture
Lève l'ancre pour une exotique nature!
Un Ennui, désolé par les cruels espoirs,
Croit encore à l'adieu suprême des mouchoirs!
Et, peut-être, les mâts, invitant les orages
Sont-ils de ceux qu'un vent penche sur les naufrages
Perdus, sans mâts, sans mâts, ni fertiles îlots...
Mais, ô mon cœur, entends le chant des matelots!

STÉPHANE MALLARMÉ
(1842-98)

Breeze from the Sea

The body's sad, and I've read everything.
To get away...! I have the itchy wing
Of the migrator: foreign surf and skies!
Europe's old gardens in reflecting eyes
Can't hold me back – such drenches of the sea
These nights! – nor my lamp's fruitless clarity
On the empty page too white to be possessed,
Nor the young wife, her baby at her breast.
I'm leaving! Schooner, balancing your spars,
Weigh anchor for some world with different stars!
This living boredom, hurt with hope, believes
Still in the last goodbye of handkerchieves!
Perhaps these storm-inviting masts are due
To bend until a gale has wrecked them too –
No masts, no fecund isles, no anything –
But heart, just listen: how the sailors sing!

STÉPHANE MALLARMÉ

«Demain, dès l'aube...»

Demain, dès l'aube, à l'heure où blanchit la campagne,
Je partirai. Vois-tu, je sais que tu m'attends.
J'irai par la forêt, j'irai par la montagne.
Je ne puis demeurer loin de toi plus longtemps.

Je marcherai les yeux fixés sur mes pensées,
Sans rien voir au dehors, sans entendre aucun bruit,
Seul, inconnu, le dos courbé, les mains croisées,
Triste, et le jour pour moi sera comme la nuit.

Je ne regarderai ni l'or du soir qui tombe,
Ni les voiles au loin descendant vers Harfleur,
Et quand j'arriverai, je mettrai sur ta tombe
Un bouquet de houx vert et de bruyère en fleur.

VICTOR HUGO
(1802-85)

'At dawn tomorrow'

At dawn tomorrow, time of whitening fields,
I'll start. You see, I know you're waiting for me.
I'll go through woods, I'll go by hill and dale.
I can no longer bear to keep away.

I'll walk with eyes on nothing but my thoughts,
No world outside to hear or see at all,
Alone, unknown, back bent, hands crossed behind,
Sorrowing: day shall be for me as night.

I shall not watch the gold of evening fall
Or distant sails dropping towards Harfleur,
And when I'm there, I'll lay upon your grave
Green holly, flowering heather: my bouquet.

VICTOR HUGO

Autre Éventail
(de Mademoiselle Mallarmé)

O rêveuse, pour que je plonge
Au pur délice sans chemin,
Sache, par un subtil mensonge,
Garder mon aile dans ta main.

Une fraîcheur de crépuscule
Te vient à chaque battement
Dont le coup prisonnier recule
L'horizon délicatement.

Vertige! voici que frissonne
L'espace comme un grand baiser
Qui, fou de naître pour personne,
Ne peut jaillir ni s'apaiser.

Sens-tu le paradis farouche
Ainsi qu'un rire enseveli
Se couler du coin de ta bouche
Au fond de l'unanime pli!

Le sceptre des rivages roses
Stagnants sur les soirs d'or, ce l'est,
Ce blanc vol fermé que tu poses
Contre le feu d'un bracelet.

STÉPHANE MALLARMÉ
(1842-98)

Another Fan

(Mademoiselle Mallarmé's)

Dear dreamer, help me to take off
Into my pathless, pure delight,
By always holding in your glove
My wing, a thin pretence of flight.

A freshness as of twilight brushes
Against you as you flutter me,
And each imprisoned wing-beat pushes
Back the horizon tenderly.

It's dizzying: shivers run through space
Like an enormous kiss, which, mad
At being born for no one's face,
Can not discharge, nor yet subside.

Don't you feel heaven is shy? It slips,
Blushing, a piece of laughter stifled,
Down by the corner of your lips
To hide in my concerted fold.

This sceptre rules the banks of rose
And pools of evening's golden mire,
This flying whiteness that you close
And land beside a bracelet's fire.

STÉPHANE MALLARMÉ

«Jeanne était au pain sec»

Jeanne était au pain sec dans le cabinet noir,
Pour un crime quelconque, et, manquant au devoir,
J'allai voir la proscrite en pleine forfaiture,
Et lui glissai dans l'ombre un pot de confiture
Contraire aux lois. Tous ceux sur qui, dans ma cité,
Repose le salut de la société,
S'indignèrent, et Jeanne a dit d'une voix douce:
– Je ne toucherai plus mon nez avec mon pouce;
Je ne me ferai plus griffer par le minet.
Mais on s'est récrié: – Cette enfant vous connaît;
Elle sait à quel point vous êtes faible et lâche.
Elle vous voit toujours rire quand on se fâche.
Pas de gouvernement possible. A chaque instant
L'ordre est troublé par vous; le pouvoir se détend;
Plus de règle. L'enfant n'a plus rien qui l'arrête.
Vous démolissez tout. – Et j'ai bassé la tête,
Et j'ai dit: – Je n'ai rien a répondre à cela,
J'ai tort. Oui, c'est avec ces indulgences-là
Qu'on a toujours conduit les peuples à leur perte.
Qu'on me mette au pain sec. – Vous le méritez, certe,
On vous y mettra. – Jeanne alors, dans son coin noir,
M'a dit tout bas, levant ses yeux si beaux à voir,
Pleins de l'autorité des douces créatures:
– Eh bien, moi, je t'irai porter des confitures.

VICTOR HUGO
(1802-85)

'Jeanne was on bread and water'

Jeanne was on bread and water in a dark room
For some dark crime; but I could not conform
To duty, I visited the outlaw in the gloom
And slipped her underhand a pot of jam
Against the regulations. Those who in my city
See to the health of our society
Were not amused. Jeanne meekly promised them,
'I'll stop making that rude sign with my thumb;
I won't make Pussy scratch me any more.'
But they protested, 'That child has got your measure;
She knows how weak and soft you are. She sees
You always laugh, when everybody's cross.
How can we govern her? Behind our backs
You interfere with order, power goes slack,
Law breaks down: the child's left to run unchecked.
You're ruining everything.' I hung my head
And said, 'I've nothing to say in my defence.
I'm in the wrong. Paternalism and indulgence
Have always led to the downfall of a people.
Put me on bread and water.' 'Indeed we will –
You deserve it.' Jeanne at this, from her dark place,
Said to me quietly, raising those dear eyes
That have the authority of the sweet and harmless:
'Well, anyway, I shall come and bring you jam.'

VICTOR HUGO

Les Joujoux de la Morte

La petite Marie est morte,
Et son cercueil est si peu long
Qu'il tient sous le bras qui l'emporte
Comme un étui de violon.

Sur le tapis et sur la table
Traîne l'héritage enfantin.
Les bras ballants, l'air lamentable,
Tout affaissé, gît le pantin.

Et si la poupée est plus ferme,
C'est la faute de son bâton;
Dans son œil une larme germe,
Un soupir gonfle son carton.

Une dînette abandonnée
Mêle ses plats de bois verni
À la troupe désarçonnée
Des écuyers de Franconi.

La boîte à musique est muette;
Mais, quand on pousse le ressort
Où se posait sa main fluette,
Un murmure plaintif en sort.

L'émotion chevrote et tremble
Dans: *Ah! vous dirai-je, maman!*
Le *Quadrille des Lanciers* semble
Triste comme un enterrement,

Et des pleurs vous mouillent la joue
Quand *la Donna è mobile*,
Sur le rouleau qui tourne et joue,
Expire avec un son filé.

Le cœur se navre à ce mélange
Puérilement douloureux,
Joujoux d'enfant laissés par l'ange,
Berceau que la tombe a fait creux!

THÉOPHILE GAUTIER
(1811-72)

Her Toys

My little friend Marie has died;
Her coffin is so short and thin
It goes under the bearer's arm
Like the case of a violin.

Over the carpet and the table
Her childish legacy is scattered.
Here lies the jumping-jack, prostrate
With dangling arms, completely shattered.

The puppet bears up rather better,
Thanks to the stick you hold her by;
But on her eye a tear has seeded,
Her cardboard's swollen with a sigh.

A dinner-service for the dolls,
In varnished wood with several courses,
Lies jumbled with a circus troupe
Who've fallen off Franconi's horses.

The music-box says nothing now,
But if you find and press the spring
Where she once set her slender thumb,
It starts a plaintive murmuring.

What feelings shake and quaver through
'Oh mummy, I shall tell you all!' –
And the quadrille of lancers sounds
As gloomy as a funeral.

But the tears pour across your cheek
When 'La Donna è mobile',
Played by the roller whirling round,
Slowly runs down and dies away.

The heart breaks over the disorder
Of childhood in this painful room:
Toys that the angel has abandoned;
The cradle emptied in the tomb.

Théophile Gautier

La Jeune Morte

Qui que tu sois, Vivant, passe vite parmi
L'herbe du tertre où gît ma cendre inconsolée;
Ne foule point les fleurs de l'humble mausolée
D'où j'écoute ramper le lierre et la fourmi.

Tu t'arrêtes? Un chant de colombe a gémi.
Non! qu'elle ne soit pas sur ma tombe immolée!
Si tu veux m'être cher, donne-lui la volée.
La vie est si douce, ah! laisse-la vivre, ami.

Le sais-tu? sous le myrte enguirlandant la porte,
Épouse et vierge, au seuil nuptial, je suis morte,
Si proche et déjà loin de celui que j'aimais.

Mes yeux se sont fermés à la lumière heureuse,
Et maintenant j'habite, hélas! et pour jamais,
L'inexorable Erèbe et la Nuit Ténébreuse.

JOSÉ-MARIA DE HEREDIA
(1842-1905)

A Young Dead Woman

No matter who you are, you are alive: pass quickly
  Among the grasses by my humble vault:
  Don't crush the flowers where I lie unconsoled
  Listening to the climbing ant and ivy.

I think you stopped. That singing was a dove: it moaned.
  Oh no, don't sacrifice it on my tomb.
  To earn my favour, give it flight and freedom.
  Life is so sweet: oh, let it live, my friend.

  It was under the myrtle garland, at the door,
  On the sill of marriage I died, a virgin wife,
So near – already far from him I used to love.

  So my eyes closed against the happy light.
  And now I stay – alas, for evermore –
With Erebus deaf to prayers, in the embrace of Night.

JOSÉ-MARIA DE HEREDIA

Le pinson d'E...

C'est très miraculeux: ce pinson si joli
Qui sautillait d'un air attentif et poli
Tout au bout des barreaux, prêtant sa tête fine
À ma bouche lui sifflant l'air de la *Czarine*,
Il n'est plus! Le voici sans souffle désormais.
Il avait bien souffert, autant que tu l'aimais!
Maussade, hélas! et symptôme bien pire encore,
Immobile et muet dans la cage sonore
Du pépiement des autres «hôtes de nos bois»
Et vibrante Dieu sait comme de leurs émois,
De leurs ébats plus fous que les jeux de la houle.
Il s'était accroupi, se contournant en boule,
La tête sous son aile, ayant l'air de dormir,
Et tu gardais l'espoir, cessant de trop gémir,
De le croire en effet endormi...La nuit sombre
Vint, qui nous consola quelque peu. Mais quand l'ombre
Se dissipa, cédant, Soleil, à ton effort,
La vérité nous apparut: il était mort!
Tu reculas d'horreur malgré tout ton courage
Ordinaire, et n'osais le sortir de la cage.
J'accomplis en ton lieu ce douloureux devoir.
Et toi, dépliant en silence un vieux *Chat noir*,
Le replias sur le cadavre avec des larmes,
Linceul approprié, symbole non sans charmes!
Nous débattîmes un long temps l'heure et le lieu
Où rendre les derniers honneurs au petit dieu.
Tout à coup tu pris ton panier déjà célèbre
Et partis sans me prévenir du lieu funèbre
Destiné dans ton cœur à l'enterrement dû,
Emportant en ce «char» l'oiseau, bien entendu.
Quand tu revins, t'avais l'air fier et plein de grâce
De quelqu'un ayant fait, sans bruit et sans grimace,
Ce qu'on peut appeler une grande action:
«Je l'ai jeté dans les caveaux du Panthéon!»
T'écrias-tu, – puis, car la femme est toujours femme,
Et tes yeux éteignant soudain leur sombre flamme,
Tu repris, et cela me parut aussi beau:
«Il aurait peut-être mieux fait sur mon chapeau!»

PAUL VERLAINE (1844-96)

E's Finch

Incredible: that pretty finch of E's
That hopped with such attentive courtesies
Right to the bars, his delicate head oblique
To judge 'the Czarine' whistled by my beak –
He's no more. There, he's out of breath for good.
He'd suffered, though you loved him all you could –
Moping – oh God! – and – a still worse presage –
Mute and immobile in the noisy cage
Wild with the woodnotes of our other guests
And shaken with the throbbing of their breasts,
Their fluttery games that crash like waves at play.
He'd crouched down in a ball, head cleared away
Under his wing, as if he were asleep.
And you, not weeping too much now, could keep
Up hope, believing that he slept. Dark night
Came, with some consolation. But when light
Pushed back the yielding shadow from our bed,
The truth was made too manifest: he was dead.
You shrank in horror, though you're not without
Courage; and didn't dare to get him out:
A painful duty for you. I did that.
You opened silently an old *Black Cat*;
In tears you closed it round the corpse, a neat
And charmingly symbolic winding-sheet.
We argued ages, when to give, and where,
Last honours to the little god of air.
Suddenly you took your basket (known to fame
Before) and left, not letting on the name
Of where you fancied having him interred,
But carrying in the mourning *Cat* the bird.
When you came back, looking as virtuous
As someone who, without a scowl or fuss,
Has done a moral masterpiece in one,
You cried: 'I threw him in the Pantheon.'
And then, eternal female all the same,
Abruptly turning off your eyes' dark flame
You added this, as bright a mot as that:
'Perhaps he'd have gone better on my hat!'

PAUL VERLAINE

À Madame du Châtelet

Si vous voulez que j'aime encore,
Rendez-moi l'âge des amours;
Au crépuscule de mes jours
Rejoignez, s'il se peut, l'aurore.

Des beaux lieux où le dieu du vin
Avec l'Amour tient son empire,
Le Temps, qui me prend par la main,
M'avertit que je me retire.

De son inflexible rigueur
Tirons au moins quelque avantage,
Qui n'a pas l'esprit de son âge
De son âge a tout le malheur.

Laissons à la belle jeunesse
Ses folâtres emportements:
Nous ne vivons que deux moments;
Qu'il en soit un pour la sagesse.

Quoi! pour toujours vous me fuyez,
Tendresse, illusion, folie,
Dons du ciel, qui me consoliez
Des amertumes de la vie!

On meurt deux fois, je le vois bien:
Cesser d'aimer et d'être aimable,
C'est une mort insupportable;
Cesser de vivre, ce n'est rien.

Ainsi je déplorais la perte
Des erreurs de mes premiers ans;
Et mon âme, aux désirs ouverte,
Regrettait ses égarements.

Du ciel alors daignant descendre,
L'Amitié vint à mon secours;
Elle était peut-être aussi tendre,
Mais moins vive que les Amours.

To Madame du Châtelet

If you want me to love again,
Give me that age when love is born,
And to the twilight of my days
Attach, if that can be, the dawn.

From the fair places where the god
Of wine, with Venus' son, holds sway,
Time, who has caught me by the hand,
Gives notice I must come away.

From his unbending stiffness draw
At least some benefit for us:
To lack the spirit of one's age
Means suffering its unhappiness.

Abandon to the lovely young
Their rather foolish ecstasies.
We have in life just two good times:
Let's reserve one for being wise.

Oh! will they leave me now for ever?
All softness, every dream and folly?
Those gifts of heaven, which consoled me
Against sour truths and melancholy!

I see we die not once, but twice:
And the insufferable death
Is when our time for loving ends;
I scarcely mind the end of breath.

So I was mourning for the loss
Of those mistakes of some years back,
Still open to desire, recalling
Sadly my ventures off the track –

When Friendship, kindly leaving heaven,
Came down to help me from above;
She had perhaps the tenderness,
But not the liveliness of Love.

Touché de sa beauté nouvelle,
Et de sa lumière éclairé,
Je la suivis; mais je pleurai
De ne pouvoir plus suivre qu'elle.

VOLTAIRE
(1694-1778)

Touched by her beauty strange and new,
Enlightened by her glow of mind,
I followed her; but wept that I
Had no one else to walk behind.

VOLTAIRE

Colloque sentimental

Dans le vieux parc solitaire et glacé,
Deux formes ont tout à l'heure passé.

Leurs yeux sont morts et leurs lèvres sont molles,
Et l'on entend à peine leurs paroles.

Dans le vieux parc solitaire et glacé,
Deux spectres ont évoqué le passé.

– Te souvient-il de notre extase ancienne?
– Pourquoi voulez-vous donc qu'il m'en souvienne?

– Ton coeur bat-il toujours à mon seul nom?
Toujours vois-tu mon âme en rêve? – Non.

– Ah! les beaux jours de bonheur indicible
Où nous joignions nos bouches! – C'est possible.

– Qu'il était bleu, le ciel, et grand, l'espoir!
– L'espoir a fui, vaincu, vers le ciel noir.

Tels ils marchaient dans les avoines folles,
Et la nuit seule entendit leurs paroles.

PAUL VERLAINE
(1844-96)

An Exchange of Feelings

In the old park, deserted in the frost,
A while ago two shapes came drifting past.

Their eyes have died, their lips become so weak
That you can hardly hear a word they speak.

In the old park, deserted in the frost,
A ghost was reminiscing to a ghost.

– Can you recall our ecstasy of long ago?
– Why stir the memory? Why do you want to know?

– Does your heart beat at just my name, as ever?
Do you still see my spirit in your dreams? – No. Never.

– O lovely days of speechless happiness
When our mouths met! – Speechless? Perhaps it was.

– How blue the sky was and what hopes we had!
– Hope ran away to the black sky, defeated.

So they walk on in the self-seeding grass
With only night to hear them as they pass.

PAUL VERLAINE

92.

Colloque sentimental

—

Dans le vieux parc solitaire et glacé
Deux formes ont tout-à-l'heure passé.

Leurs yeux sont morts et leurs lèvres sont molles
Et l'on entend à peine leurs paroles.

Dans le vieux parc solitaire et glacé
Deux spectres ont évoqué le passé:

– « Te souvient il de notre extase ancienne ?
– « Pourquoi voulez vous donc qu'il m'en souvienne ! »

– « Ton cœur bat-il toujours à mon seul nom ?
~~C_____ ___ ____ _____ à tu mon ____?~~ – « Non.
« Toujours vois tu mon âme en rêve —
                                   – « Ah ! les beaux

Notes

The French texts printed here are taken from standard editions. I am most grateful to my friend Marion Maitlis for queries on many points in my versions. All errors however are my own.

FRENCH VERSE

A word on French prosody might be useful. French is not an accentual language and its poetry does not work by stresses and feet as English verse does. A traditional French poet had three main points to consider when writing a line:

1. The typical line (an "Alexandrine") is simply twelve syllables long. When counting, you also count the mute *e* at the end of a word (*-e* or *-es*), as with Chaucer; except that *-e* elides and doesn't count if the next word starts with a vowel or *h*. (In southern France speakers still pronounce these final *es*, but not elsewhere.)

2. In a line this length there is a pause, a word-break, or more often a phrase-break (a caesura), after syllable six. For example:

> La chair est triste, hélas! et j'ai lu tous les livres.

Here *triste* looks like two syllables, but the mute *e* elides away before the *h* of *hélas* (and the caesura comes there, at the exclamation mark). Thus the line consists of two bits of language, each six syllables long. Actually, however, *livres* provides a twelfth and a thirteenth syllable, which brings us to the next point.

3. Rhymes must "alternate" (a technical term) between "masculine" and "feminine" (where there's an extra syllable at the line-end provided by a mute e). Thus in the poem quoted ('Brise marine' by Mallarmé) the rhymes go *'livres/ivres, cieux/yeux, trempe/lampe, défend/enfant, mature/nature'* and so on.

The alternation of masculine and feminine rhymes occurs in all kinds of French verse. The fixed caesura, however, is only expected in Alexandrines.

Of course, these are the rules of *traditional* versification – they have been under various forms of attack for a century. The rules can be played with, as in Verlaine's 'Nevermore' in this book, a sonnet which starts with four identical feminine rhymes and goes on with four identical masculine rhymes; and in his Lesbian sonnets, 'Les amies', all the rhymes are feminine.

Only two poems in this book do not conform to the rules described above: 'Renaud le tueur de femmes' (which is a popular ballad) and Laforgue's 'Solo de Lune' (which is in *vers libre* – for further comment see below).

COMMENTS

14-17. **Le Manchy**: Leconte de Lisle's poem is about his cousin, who had a black grandparent. This is why he describes her as 'rosy' (meaning she looked 'white') but full of 'native' grace. (The point is made less openly, behind a cliché, in the original.) He fell in love with this beautiful girl and told his mother he wanted to marry her, and his mother fainted. The place is Réunion, the island in the Indian Ocean where the poet was born and brought up.

20-23. **Renaud le tueur de femmes**: The French for 'lady-killer' (an early nineteenth-century "humorous" word) is 'tombeur de femmes'. But Renaud was a literal killer, like Bluebeard. (The tune for this ballad has been reproduced at the end of the poem.)

26-29. **Thyrsis and Amaranta**: I have cut some merely dedicatory lines from the beginning of La Fontaine's poem, addressed to La Rochefoucauld's beautiful niece, Mademoiselle de Sillery, who had complained his *Contes* were hard to understand. Perhaps she was too innocent for them.

30-33. **Le Tombeau de Marmousette**: Many of Saint-Amant's near-contemporaries wrote such poems about pets, but the theme is time-honoured and goes at least from Catullus ('Passer, deliciae mcac puellae') to Corbière ('Sonnet à Sir Bob'). Musette means 'bagpipe', but here the context forces one to think 'little Muse' as well. In the English, 'spick and span' is partly in memory of Virginia Woolf's spaniel biography *Flush*. The game, by the way, was not actually croquet but Mall (as played at one time in Pall-Mall).

34-35. **Sonnets pour Hélène**: In the second (more famous) sonnet, *ombres myrteux* (masculine) means lovers' ghosts because the myrtle tree is sacred to Venus.

40-41. **«Elle était déchaussée, elle était décoiffée»**: Hugo's poem is no.XXI in Livre I, 'Aurore', of his book *Les Contemplations* (1856).

44-45. **Les Pas**. Valéry's poem has a curious (and untranslatable) change of person in it, from *tu* to *vous*. I have found no critic brave enough to hazard a guess at what this means. My guess is that *tu* is Valéry's way of addressing in his mind the idealised absent person, and *vous* is the actual present person who has now reached his bedside. It might be thought that this person called *vous* cannot (yet) be an intimate (i.e., is not Valéry's wife); but it is, or at least used to be, usual for French husbands to call their wives *vous*, certainly in public.

46-47. **Élégie** XIX: Ronsard's nineteenth 'Élégie' is partly based on a kiss-poem in Latin by the contemporary Dutch poet Johannes Secundus ('Basia XIII'). That is, Ronsard uses the first 12 lines of his model, then departs from it completely. "Basia XIII" continues with Charon taking the poet's soul away to Hades and the girl sharing hers with her lover to keep him alive, two bodies with one soul.

58-59. **«Non que je veuille ôter la liberté»**: Pernette du Guillet was the innocent recipient of Scève's *Délie* poems. She died young and her poems were published posthumously by her husband.

60-67. **Solo de lune**: Laforgue's poem, which is in what the French call *vers libre* (with rhymes, often not obeying the strict rules, but no metre), is no.VII in a connected group entitled by editors 'Derniers Poèmes' (but the group is really one poem in movements, like a musical suite). It was written in the summer of 1886, and the quatrains buried in it are cannibalised from 'Arabesques de Malheur', a poem of a more traditional type written earlier that year: the clash of the two styles of writing gives a kind of actuality and richness to the colloquial journey-poem. 'Arabesques de Malheur' was only published after Laforgue's death, and would presumably have been suppressed by him as a worked-out object if he had lived, in spite of its being a good poem.

Readers who wonder what happened may care to know that this girl Laforgue was unable (through poverty) to declare himself to, much less propose to, was English, named Leah Lee, and they did marry, on the last day of that year, in a Kensington church. (See David Arkell's biography of Laforgue.) Both died of tuberculosis, he a few months, she a few years, later.

70-71. **«Demain dès l'aube»**: From *Les Contemplations*, Livre IV, 'Aujourd'hui'. The grave was that of his daughter Léopoldine, who had been drowned, together with her new husband, in 1843, the year of their marriage. Hugo learned of their deaths when reading the paper five days later in a café, on his way home from a holiday in the Pyrenees with his mistress. The poem is dated 3 September 1847.

74-75. **«Jeanne était au pain sec»**: Jeanne was Hugo's granddaughter, aged seven at the date of writing given – he was 74. The poem is from *L'Art d'Être Grand-Père*, and is dated 21 October 1876.

76-77. **Les Joujoux de la Morte**: Gautier had a long liaison, almost a marriage, with Ernesta Grisi, an Italian singer. He wrote the scenario of *Giselle* for her ballerina sister, Carlotta; and her other sister, Giulia, an opera-singer and actress, was the mother of the dead child in this poem. Gautier was, then, a sort of uncle to the child.

78-79. **La Jeune Morte**: Heredia's young dead woman is an ancient Roman, and the poem is (like the Antony and Cleopatra one) a unit from his world-historical sonnet-book *Les Trophées* (1893). Robert Lowell included versions of some of these in his own sonnet-book *History*.

80-81. **Le pinson d'E...**: Verlaine adds domesticity of a sort to the tradition of mistress'-pet poems. 'E' was Eugénie Krantz, the whore with whom Verlaine was living when he died. Her basket is 'known to fame' because he had put it in poems before. The phrase in quotes in line 9 is from La Fontaine's second fable, 'Le Corbeau et le Renard'. I felt the best way to cope with this was to use an equally famous English phrase (from 'L'Allegro'). Further down, there is an untranslatable pun about the literary magazine *Le Chat Noir*: 'char funèbre' is the French for hearse. The poem is dated 20 February 1893.

82-83. **À Madame du Châtelet**: Voltaire was only 46 when he wrote this poem to his mistress. It seems a bit premature.

ACKNOWLEDGEMENTS

I am grateful to the editors of *Margin* and the *London Magazine*, where some of these versions first appeared.

Acknowledgement is also due to Éditions Gallimard for free permission to print the one text that is in copyright, Paul Valéry's 'Les Pas', and to Princeton University Press and to Routledge who have translation rights in Valéry's *Collected Works* for, respectively, the USA & Canada and the rest of the world. The *Poems* volume of this was translated by David Paul. It is out of print.

Chronological Table

1501?-64? Maurice Scève.

1520?-45 Pernette du Guillet.

1522-60 Joachim du Bellay.

1524-85 Pierre de Ronsard.

1556 Ronsard in a poem alludes to his friends as the Pléiade.

1572 Massacre of Huguenots on St Bartholomew's Day.

1594-1661 Saint-Amant.

1601?-55 Tristan l'Hermite.

1621-95 La Fontaine.

1636 *Le Cid* (P. Corneille, 1606-84).

1659 *Les précieuses ridicules* (Molière, 1622-73).

1661 Louis XIV, le Roi Soleil (1638-1715, king since 1643), begins actually ruling, on the death of Mazarin.

1667 *Andromaque* (Racine, 1639-99).

1694-1778 Voltaire.

1697 *Contes de ma mère l'Oye* (Perrault's fairy tales).

1751-65 *Encyclopédie*, ed. Diderot (1713-84) & d'Alembert (1717-83)

1759-81 Diderot's art criticism (*Les Salons*).

1762 *Du contrat social* (J.-J. Rousseau, 1712-78).

1789 La Révolution, beginning the First Republic (till 1804).

1793-94 The Terror, the period between 17 September 1793 and the fall of Robespierre the following 27 July, during which nearly 20,000 people were executed in France, including the poet André Chénier (1762-94) on 25 July.

1795-99 Le Directoire.

1798 Napoleon (1769-1821) conquers Egypt.

1799 Napoleon made First Consul (with dictatorial powers).

1804 Napoleon makes himself Emperor (i.e. First Empire starts).

1802-85 Victor Hugo.

1808-55 Gérard de Nerval.

1810-57 Alfred de Musset.

1811-72 Théophile Gautier.

1814 Allies invade France; Napoleon exiled to Elba.

1815 Waterloo (June 18).

1818-94 Leconte de Lisle.

1821-67 Charles Baudelaire.

1824-30 Charles X (1757-1836) last absolute king of France.

1829 *Les Chouans* (first success of Balzac, 1799-1850).

1830 *Hernani* (play by Victor Hugo): its first two performances, on February 25 and 27, are riotous confrontations between the traditionalists and the Romantics.

1830 The July Revolution, followed by Louis-Philippe ruling as constitutional monarch till 1848.

1838 Daguerre makes his first daguerrotypes.

1839 *La Chartreuse de Parme* (Stendhal, 1783-1842).

1842-1905 José-Maria de Heredia.

1842-98 Stéphane Mallarmé.

1844-96 Paul Verlaine.

1845, 1846 & 1859 Salons (art shows) reviewed by Baudelaire.

1848 Revolution, followed by Second Republic (1848-52).

1852-70 Second Empire (Napoleon III).

1854-91 Arthur Rimbaud.

1857 *Madame Bovary* (Flaubert, 1821-80).

1860-87 Jules Laforgue.

1863 Manet's *Déjeuner sur l'herbe* causes a sensation at the Salon des refusés.

1866, 1871 & 1876 *Le Parnasse contemporain*, three series.

1867 *Thérèse Raquin* (Zola, 1840-1902)

1870-71 The Franco-Prussian War

1870 The September Revolution ends Napoleon III's empire and begins the Third Republic (which ends in 1940).

1871 The Commune in Paris.

1871-1945 Paul Valéry.

1874 The word Impressionist is invented to ridicule an exhibition of work by Morisot, Pissarro, Cézanne, Degas, Renoir, and Monet, held in the photographer Nadar's studio.

1884 *Les Poètes Maudits* (by Verlaine) draws attention to the work of Rimbaud, Corbière, Mallarmé, Lautréamont and others.

1894-1906 The Dreyfus Affair.

1895 First public performance of the Cinématographe (invented by the Lumière brothers) in Paris.

FRENCH POETRY FROM BLOODAXE
FRENCH-ENGLISH PARALLEL TEXT SELECTIONS

JEAN TARDIEU *The River Underground: Selected Poems & Prose*
Translated by David Kelley, with drawings by Picasso
Tardieu's 'Theatre of the Absurd' anticipated Beckett and Ionesco.
His poetry has an almost childlike simplicity, and in France he is
studied in both universities and primary schools. 208 pages: £6.95 paper.

PIERRE REVERDY *Selected Poems*
Translated by John Ashbery, Mary Ann Caws & Germaine Brée
Edited by Timothy Bent & Germaine Brée
Pierre Reverdy (1889-1960) is one of the greatest and most influential
figures in modern French poetry. Breton hailed him in his Surrealist
Manifesto as 'the greatest poet of the time'. 180 pages: £7.95 paper.

BLOODAXE CONTEMPORARY FRENCH POETS
FRENCH-ENGLISH PARALLEL TEXT SINGLE COLLECTIONS
Series Editors: Timothy Mathews & Michael Worton

1. YVES BONNEFOY *Du Mouvement et de l'immobilité de Douve:*
On the Motion and Immobility of Douve
Translated by Galway Kinnell, introduction by Timothy Mathews
Bonnefoy is a central figure in post-war French culture. In *Douve*
(1953), his first book of poetry, he reflects on the value and mecha-
nism of language in a series of variations on the life and death of
a much loved woman, Douve. 192 pages: £7.95 paper (January 1992).

2. RENÉ CHAR *Les Matinaux: The Dawn Breakers*
Edited & translated by Michael Worton
The poetry of René Char (1907-88) confronts the major 20th century
moral, political and artistic concerns with a simplicity of vision and
expression inspired by the poet-philosophers of Ancient Greece.
Published after the War, *Les Matinaux* looks forward to a better
and freer world, and includes some of the finest love poems ever
written in French. 160 pages: £7.95 paper (January 1992).

3. HENRI MICHAUX *Déplacements Dégagements: Spaced, Displaced*
Translated by David & Helen Constantine, introduction by Peter Broome
Henri Michaux (1899-1984) travelled from the Amazon to the Far
East, and into the strange hinterland of his own inner space. His
last book has poetry testing itself dangerously at the frontiers, acut-
ely analytical, full of surprising insights into previously undiscovered
movements of the mind. 192 pages: £7.95 paper (January 1992).

Forthcoming: 4. AIMÉ CÉSAIRE *Cahier d'un retour au pays natal: Notebook of a
Return to My Native Land,* translated by Mireille Rosario & Annie Pritchard.
5. ANNE HÉBERT *Le tombeau des rois: The Tomb of the Kings,* translated by
Joanne Collie & Anne Hébert.